The Commission

First published in 2009 by
THE AMERICAN POLICY ROUNDTABLE
National Headquarters
11288 Alameda Drive
Strongsville, Ohio 44149

For more information about the American Policy
Roundtable log on to www.APRoundtable.org.

ISBN: 978-0-9779632-2-5

Unless otherwise indicated, Bible quotations are taken
from The New International Version of the Bible.
Copyright (c) 1978 by the International Bible Society.

Table of Contents

"If your cause is just, you may look with confidence to the Lord, and entreat him to plead it as his own. ... There is not a single instance in history, in which civil liberty was lost, and religious liberty preserved entire. If, therefore, we yield up our temporal property, we at the same time deliver the conscience into bondage."

Rev. John Witherspoon, May 17th 1776

Signer of the Declaration of Independence
President of Princeton College
Mentor to James Madison

Introduction

This book is a bit unusual. It begins with a very wide angle shot of American history. It ends with some very specific personal advice for people of faith in this current crisis. This approach is intentional.

Critics on the Left will be strongly tempted to take phrases from this book out of context to blunt the effect of this discussion of principle. Such is to be expected. One thing must be made clear from the start, however. Nothing in this book suggests that the role of civil government in America includes the right to judge matters of conscience. Decisions of personal faith or disbelief are outside the sphere of civil government both in principle and law.

In addition, a biblical approach to personal faith comes without the need for compulsion in any fashion. The Bible forces matters of faith and conscience upon no one. America has always honored this bedrock principle and should never cease to do so. Should someone ask what is it that Christian people want from America, the answer is quite simple: A country where people voluntarily honor the principles of the Declaration of Independence and the Constitution as it stands today.

There is an old story often retold about a child born to nobility who somehow loses her way. One day she awakens far from the home of her birth—confused, cold and very alone. Mistaken in her identity she is forced to live as a pauper with the memories of a princess. The rest of the story is about the adventures she encounters trying to make her way back home. Such is the story of America's children in the 21st century. We are walking in a deeply troubled age a long, long way from the place our parents and grandparents once called home.

This work is submitted to a troubled nation in the hope of rediscovering the pathway home.

~

Section One
The Constitution:
What the Founders Left Us

No one wrote the screenplay for America. America did not begin as a nation or even a state. America began with a few boats of cold and lonely Pilgrims longing to be free. America is a puzzle of pieces and parts that came together over generations of struggle. It is the story of very imperfect people longing to be free, learning to live together in liberty under law. At its point of origin America is a set of ideas.

The first settlers of the 1600s came to build communities based on "compacts" or "covenants." The first and most famous of these is the Mayflower Compact, which was signed in 1620. It is a pretty small document but carried within it are the seeds of civil government in America. This is how the first governmental agreement in America read:

In the name of God, Amen. We, whose names are underwritten, the Loyal Subjects of our dread Sovereign Lord, King James, by the Grace of God, of England, France and Ireland, King, Defender of the Faith, & Having undertaken for the Glory of God, and Advancement of the Christian Faith, and the Honour of our King and Country, a voyage to plant the first colony in the northern parts of Virginia; do by these presents, solemnly and mutually in the Presence of God and one of another, covenant and combine ourselves together into a civil Body Politick, for our better Ordering and Preservation, and Furtherance of the Ends aforesaid; And by Virtue hereof to enact, constitute, and frame, such just and equal Laws, Ordinances, Acts, Constitutions and Offices, from time to time, as shall be thought most meet and convenient for the General good

of the Colony; unto which we promise all due
submission and obedience. In Witness whereof
we have hereunto subscribed our names at Cape
Cod the eleventh of November, in the Reign of
our Sovereign Lord, King James of England,
France and Ireland, the eighteenth, and of
Scotland the fifty-fourth. Anno Domini, 1620.

America is much like the story of the mustard seed. From a very small seed grew a very large enterprise. There is no certain evidence the earliest Pilgrims and later colonists came to these shores intent on building a nation. Their writings indicate they came instead to live out an experiment in Liberty under the sovereign protection of Great Britain. They were British citizens and held to the rights of British common law but quickly discovered things here were different. They were part of a new world.

It took over 140 years of painful experience for the Colonies to embrace the necessity of separating from Great Britain and establishing a new nation. Independence was not their first choice. Why would people who believed in the same God as their relatives back home, who shared the same names, traditions and currency want to leave the mother country and go their own way? What had changed in the mind of the body politic from 1620 to 1776?

Why the American Adventure Began

The single most important question any student must ask about America is found in a single word: "Why?" Why did they come here? Why did they stay here? Why would they attempt to start their own nation? Why were they willing to die in a struggle to be free here?

Fortunately, we don't have to guess about the answer. The answer is best summarized in the Declaration of Independence, the core document of the American enterprise. This document is the incorporation paper for the USA. Without it, nothing else makes sense. The grievances of the Colonies were outlined in this founding rationale for Independence. Before the listing of complaints began, however, the Founders carefully defined the reality of their worldview. They laid out the philosophical and practical platform for their new government.

They told us "why" with these immortal words.

IN CONGRESS, July 4, 1776.

The unanimous Declaration of the thirteen united States of America,

When in the Course of human events, it becomes necessary for one people to dissolve the political bands which have connected them with another, and to assume among the powers of the earth, the separate and equal station to which the Laws of Nature and of Nature's God entitle them, a decent respect to the opinions of mankind requires that they should declare the causes which impel them to the separation.

We hold these truths to be self-evident, that all men are created equal, that they are endowed by their Creator with certain unalienable Rights, that among these are Life, Liberty and the pursuit of Happiness.--That to secure these rights, Governments are instituted among Men, deriving their just powers from the consent of the governed, -- That whenever any Form of Government becomes destructive of these ends, it is the Right of the People to alter or to abolish it, and to institute new Government, laying its foundation on such principles and organizing its powers in such form, as to them shall seem most likely to effect their Safety and Happiness. Prudence, indeed, will dictate that Governments long established should not be changed for light and transient causes; and accordingly all experience hath shewn, that mankind are more disposed to suffer, while evils are sufferable, than to right themselves by abolishing the forms to which they are accustomed. But when a long train of abuses and usurpations, pursuing invariably the same Object evinces a design to reduce them under absolute Despotism, it is their right, it is their duty, to throw off such Government, and to provide new Guards for their future security.--Such has been the patient sufferance of these Colonies; and such is now the necessity which constrains them to alter their former Systems of Government. The history of the present King of Great Britain is a history of repeated injuries and usurpations, all having in direct object the establishment of an absolute Tyranny over these States. To prove this, let Facts be submitted to a candid world...

So Who is America For?

The ideas that define America were designed for all humankind – all who are created equal by their Creator. That was the confession of the Declaration, the foundation upon which Liberty stands. Turning that ideal into reality is the American story.

Every generation has faced the challenge of living out the Declaration of Independence. The document so boldly signed and paid for by the Founding generation is both the heart and conscience of the nation. The capacity of the founding generations to live out that confession was obviously limited. America is a story of imperfect people. The Founders had their issues, places where they fell short of the ideal. They did not permit women the right to vote. They did not permit non-land owners the right to vote. They did not foresee future challenges with Native American Indians. And they missed the critical moment of opportunity to eliminate the slave trade as Great Britain had earlier accomplished.

Acknowledging these and other failures is important. Taking them out of context, however, can lead to great error. America's Founders, in spite of their blind spots and limited capacity were the radicals of their era. They were the revolutionary catalyst in the expansion of human liberty.

It doesn't always look that way from the perspective of the 21st century. To understand how far the Declaration moved the world we have to look farther back. We have to get behind the Founders' eyes and see the world they left behind. A world divided into two classes at birth: those of privilege and everyone else. Privilege was the inheritance of those born closest to the monarchies of Europe. Everyone else was limited and somehow duty bound to a medieval obligation of service. The monarchy decided the lot, the birthright and even the religious faith of all.

The American assertion, addressed to the most powerful monarch in the word, that all men are indeed created equal by their Creator, was no small remark. Turning those words into reality was not an instant miracle, nor is it a completed work even to this day.

If America could be described as an

equation, perhaps a mathematical fraction would suit it best. The Declaration of Independence would be the common denominator. Like a fraction whose bottom figure is the number one, the root value of the Declaration must constantly be pressed into any formula for law and government. As with a fraction, no matter what kind of law, process or practice we put on the top line, it is the principles of the Declaration that remain the common denominator. We must always factor every idea by those principles.

The ideas that birthed America belong to all humankind: to the skeptic, the cynic, to the unbeliever as well as the disciple. The challenge is putting those ideas into practice in the common pursuit of liberty under law. Living out these principles has always been the true struggle.

The Ideas Behind the Constitution

Winning a war does not automatically create a nation. When the British surrendered on the field of battle, America did not suddenly take its place on the game board of life. The colonists and their Congress had managed to keep General Washington's army alive and finally victorious over the British. Next they had to figure out how to work out their independence in relationship to each other.

The period following the War for Independence was a time of transformational crisis. The British lost the War; but they did not leave the continent. France still had designs on North America. Their original Articles of Confederation had been tried by the war and found wanting. The independent colonies had to decide upon the best form of government to expand and defend their liberties. They did not turn to a powerful ruling class to take over. They did not turn to George Washington and make him king. They turned again to the transcendent ideas, the truths that had been the catalyst for independence.

What were they trying to accomplish? Where did the ideas come from? The same people who threw the tea in Boston Harbor and faced the gunfire on Lexington Green had been thinking long and hard about all of this. Leaders from Virginia, Massachusetts and

Pennsylvania had plans. They were combing the works of the ancients trying to figure out how they would govern themselves, if they were fortunate enough to have the opportunity.

Once again they called upon delegates to meet in Congress and create a document for review and ratification by the individual state legislative bodies. From this 1787 Convention in Philadelphia the Constitution emerged. It was a document created by the individual states, working in union to define a limited federal structure. The states created the federal structure of government, not the other way around. They built a model for a Constitutional Republic. The Constitution was designed to help build a structure of government to secure the rights enumerated in the Declaration of Independence.

The core ideas of the US Constitution flow from somewhere. They were not totally original thought. Fortunately the Founders did a lot of writing and most of their records remain as clear evidence. American documents are not ancient history. The originals are in the National Archives. We can find copies of James

Madison's actual notes on the Constitutional Convention on the Internet today. Knowing their thoughts is a matter of reading their words.

The Constitution is not a theological document; therefore it does not quote chapters and verses of the Bible. It was not created to define the construction of a Christian nation. The Founders understood that using the term "Christian" to modify any term other than an individual follower of Christ was inappropriate. They built a structure of civil government consistent with the principles of the Declaration, which clearly includes a full recognition of the Creator God of the Bible.

Some modern historians have tried hard to turn the construction of the Constitution into a story of secularism anchored in the period of European history and thought called the Enlightenment. They do this because many secularists today are uncomfortable with the clear testimony of faith so consistent in the Founding Era.

These historical facts of faith don't fit very well with the politics and worldviews of many modern academics. Some modernists are honest enough to admit their clear bias. Others teach a different version of the Constitution; one they construct to fit their modern secular perspective. It gives them more room to justify their ideas as American.

Modern secular historians also work hard trying to pry apart the natural union between the Declaration of Independence and the Constitution. They have to do this because the clear theistic language of the Declaration makes them terribly uncomfortable. The Founders didn't just believe in God. They believed God governed in the affairs of men. The history of the language traces back through the Protestant Reformation, which is also a very uncomfortable period of history for the secular modern educators.

The revisionists' logic is to reluctantly admit the religious content of the Declaration exists but to claim that the lack of specific religious words in the Constitution proves a radical shift in worldview during the Founding Era. It is painful to consume time writing a rebuttal to such an obviously flawed argument but any fair apologetic requires such a response. Since America, at its core, is a set of ideas, accurately understanding where those ideas came from is important.

First of all, let's take a moment and count the years from 1776, when the Declaration was signed to 1787 and the signing of the Constitution. Simple math tells us there are a brief eleven years between these two epic works. George Washington, Sam Adams, John Adams and many of the Sons of Liberty who fought and suffered through the War for Independence were still living and fully engaged. They had not become sudden apostates. Their worldview had not evaporated. The notion the two documents can be separated on basic principles based on time or radical shifting worldviews is pretty ridiculous.

Comparing the Declaration and the Constitution is definitely a case of examining apples and oranges. The Declaration is a rationale, heavily weighted on the need to answer "why" the Colonies should become free and independent nations.

The Constitution is written for a wholly

different purpose. It exists to answer "how" the independent and sovereign colonies shall unite in a legal union. The mission of the Continental Congress was equally different from the mission of the Constitutional Convention. So it is only logical that the second document should be different from the first and essentially non-repetitive. Any attempt to view these documents otherwise and interpret a radical change in cultural consensus from such a comparison just doesn't square with history.

What the Founders Thought About People

The greatest evidence for the role of biblical thought in the Constitution comes from reviewing the concepts contained within the document. The Constitution exists to create a limited form of government so as to protect basic individual rights. The ancient monarchies of Europe surely didn't start out with that premise. Why individual rights? Because in a biblical worldview, individuals have absolute value given by the Creator. A constitutional government exists to secure those rights.

Why limited government instead of no government at all? If limited government affords more liberty shouldn't the absence of government create even more liberty? The Constitutional Convention understood this as a question dealing with the very nature of humankind. They did not see people as perfect or nearly perfect or in the process of perfection. They saw people in the biblical perspective as "fallen" and prone to self-interest. Sin was a word they did not run away from. Therefore that brought very realistic expectations into their governing equations. They expected people to mess up both by accident and intent; so they tried to structure a government to protect the individual from the abuse of the single tyrant as well as a tyrannical majority. Real life experience, historical study and theological teaching, all led them to the consensus that liberty could not exist without law. James Madison said it best in the famous quotation from the Federalist Papers, "If men were angels we would need no laws."

So their objective was to piece together a

federal structure that was as limited as possible – because an unlimited federal government would be a source of temptation, corruption and eventual abuse. They had to build a system with enough power, however, to be effective for the national defense and common welfare, and to protect the states from the potential of intrastate conflict. Recognizing that all men were fallen and prone to self-interest to the point of abuse, they worked to limit the power of government in every direction.

The authority of the Constitution flows from a single source: the consent of the governed, a major tenet of the Declaration. "We the People," also called the body politic, express consent by direct participation and by representative action through elected officials. The consent of the governed is clearly a principle taught throughout the Old and New Testaments. While not exclusive to biblical thought, it is wholly consistent with the teachings of Genesis, the history of the Hebrew people and the practice of the New Testament Church. In fact a favorite text of colonial pulpits was I Samuel chapter 8, a discussion of Israel's choice of self-determination in civil government. The Founders did not cite this passage in the Constitution. They did not need to do so because they were not competing with the Sunday morning pulpit. They were building the form of a civil government on principles of transcendent truth. They were not building a church or synagogue but a civil government.

The Bill of Rights is an essential discussion of protecting the individual and the states from governmental abuse. The premise of the Bill of Rights flows from the Declaration of Independence. Government does not grant rights to the individual. Instead people assemble civil governments to secure the protection of rights endowed to them by the Creator.

Government is powerful but only because the people have empowered the government by their consent. Their consent flows from their identity as the unique creations of God who gave them their rights in the first place. God has given the people the right to Liberty and the privilege of choosing how they will govern themselves under His care. That's the founding formula that is worked out between the Constitution and the Declaration.

It is this rationale that dominated the creation of the Federal Government. The Founders came reluctantly to the assembly of a federal structure. Had they been able to live free and well protected as individual sovereign states they would have done so. They tried that path and found it insufficient. The Constitutional Convention was a wary meeting. The document created was a reluctant structure, as minimal as possible, so as to not overstep the much greater importance of self-government, family, community, and the rights of the individual states. It was only passed out of Convention and ratified by the states based upon the promise of a Bill of Rights to make certain the federal government was locked down and individual and states rights protected.

The First Amendment and Religious Practice

Congress shall make no law respecting an establishment of religion, or prohibiting the free exercise thereof; or abridging the freedom of speech, or of the press; or the right of the people peaceably to assemble, and to petition the government for a redress of grievances. (First Amendment of the United States Constitution)

The First Amendment of the Bill of Rights begins with a restriction: "Congress shall make no law ..." The prohibition contained in these words could not be more specific. The First Amendment does not begin with or contain any attempt to limit the action of individuals, states or "the Church" in America. It is a specific prohibition against Congressional action. This plain language is designed to wall off the authority of the Congress to pass any law regarding "the establishment of religion or prohibiting the free exercise thereof."

How much easier would life be today if the Founders had added just a few more words in the First Amendment so that it read:

Congress and the Judiciary shall make no law regarding the establishment of religion or prohibiting the free exercise thereof.

Of course, Congress could not do so

because the only authority for lawmaking established in the Constitution resides with the Congress (Article I). So to have attempted such a restriction on the Judicial branch would have been logically and legally meaningless because there is no constitutional authority for the Judiciary to make law in the first place.

Perhaps the addition should have been, "Congress shall make no law, nor shall the Judiciary *interpret* any law respecting the establishment of religion or prohibiting the free exercise thereof." This of course raises the logical question; if Congress cannot create a law respecting the establishment of religion then how could there be such a law for the Supreme Court, which is an appellate body, to review?

Historically speaking, it took years for the US Supreme Court to develop the doctrine of judicial review, meaning that the Court had the authority to serve as the constitutional watchdog over the US Congress. It took many more generations for the Court to develop the doctrine of "incorporation" whereby it maintains the authority to apply the federal

Constitution and the Court's precedents to the states. All of this points to the stark reality that the original intention of the First Amendment was to build a barrier against the intrusion of the federal government into the matters of faith, conscience and religious practice as well as free speech, the press, the right to assembly and to petition the government.

So how in the world did America get from the original intent of the First Amendment to the place where it is today? Hardly a year goes by without a major battle in the federal judiciary over matters of "church and state." Chronicling this progression is too long a story for this document but to make one passing comment.

The failure of the US Congress to challenge the federal judiciary on this matter has served to empower federal judges to redefine the First Amendment. The Courts have been effectively legislating from the bench and rewriting the US Constitution without the consent of the governed for years. It is neither harsh nor inaccurate to acknowledge this abdication of responsibility on the part of Congress, which has created chaos in the culture on questions of religious liberty and free speech.

The right to bear arms, a speedy trial, the protection of personal property, freedom of speech, religion and assembly are all biblical concepts lodged clearly in the US Constitution. No, the chapters and verses of biblical reference are not listed in the Constitution. Such citations are wholly unnecessary because the truths of those concepts were clearly self-evident in the Founding Era.

The Constitutional prohibition against establishing titles of privilege or nobility hearkens back to the colonial sermons pointing out the mistakes Israel made in choosing a monarchy as their form of civil government. The Founders who shared intimate experiences with the tyrannical monarchies of Europe, wanted to be certain that mistake was never made again.

A seldom discussed matter of bookkeeping in the Constitution even hearkens back to a respect for the biblical principle of honoring the Sabbath. In establishing the process for a Presidential veto of Congressional action, the Founders used a count of ten days for Presidential action, not including Sundays. This is a clear, constitutional deference to the Judeo-Christian teaching of the Sabbath. Yes, it is most certainly an incidental reference, but that only makes the point more significant. The authors would not have placed the exemption in the highest law of the land if it was not important to them. The Founders lived in a world highly respectful of Judeo-Christian principles and practices. Such practice even worked its way into the establishment of a Constitutional procedure of action. It was just natural to do things in such a manner.

There are more principles that reflect biblical teaching in the Constitution. The separation of powers as well as the balance of powers are both concepts Congress saw modeled by the biblical presbytery. The very idea of a representative form of government based upon the electoral process reveals the desire of the Founders to truly anchor the new American government in the "consent of the governed."

The Founders were very careful with

this power of electing representation to the federal government. In hindsight they were clearly too careful on the question of who should be qualified to do the voting. This does not diminish the fact they still built a strong mechanism of electoral accountability into the federal system. Such a commitment to the right to vote was revolutionary in the late 1700s.

This concept flows directly from the teachings of the Protestant Reformation, which helped "flatten" the hierarchical structure of European monarchies. The Royal classes, so often in corrupt alliance with church leaders, had spawned endless tyranny across Europe. The American form of federal government would permit no such abuses. Public officials would face a constant stream of electoral reviews and ratification forcing them to be accountable to the same people upon whose consent the American enterprise began.

Electoral accountability has permitted Americans a constant, predictable process for improving their government. Through this process Americans have expanded voting rights to all citizens. Voters have also elected members of Congress who have amended the Constitution to include the direct election of the US Senate and the right for all citizens to vote for the Presidency.

The American process of law is a well-balanced equation. It is not perfect, nor did the Founders claim it to be so. It contains within itself the process of continual improvement via the amendment and electoral process. The Founders knew nobody was perfect, therefore the work of Liberty under law would be ongoing. They knew they had left the question of slavery on the table. The Constitutional process they enacted left to others the tools to right that injustice. This method has created both freedom for the individual and a form of order to protect basic civil rights. It all works well, provided "we the people" continue to do our job of responsible citizenship.

When Benjamin Franklin left the final proceedings of the Constitutional Convention he was stopped on the street by a woman with a pervasive question. The Philadelphia convention had been closed to both the public and the press. No one knew for certain what type of government would emerge for the states to consider as a binding national model. "What type of government have you given us Mr. Franklin?" questioned the citizen of Philadelphia. "A republic Madame," was Franklin's reply to which he quickly added, "if you can keep it."

Section Two
Congress: The Tool to Keep It All Straight

When the members of the Philadelphia Convention of 1787 handed Americans the Constitution, they handed all Americans a sacred trust. The Convention had done the difficult calculations. They had factored the principles of the Declaration of Independence into the numeration of a civil government. They wrestled mightily to come away with a result that was a balanced, sustainable equation.

The US Constitution is made up of only seven articles and twenty-eight amendments. The first three articles construct the Legislative,

Executive and Judicial Branches of the federal government. It is no coincidence the Legislative Branch comes first and carries the only lawmaking authority in the government of the United States. The Congress was designed to be the voice of the people in action. It embodies the principle of the consent of the governed. It is the most important primary agency in civil government today and tragically, the one most forsaken.

Congress is how America was built. The Continental Congress birthed the Declaration of Independence and sustained America through the war. Congress passed the Northwest Ordinance and turned America into a nation of States. A Constitutional Convention acted in the form of a Congress to write the great document of 1787. Congress elected the first three Presidents, all without the existence of a single political party in Washington, D.C. All the greats served in Congress or answered her call to service.

The House of Representatives was designed to work as a constant stream of citizen interplay with frequent elections every two years. The House was to be the body closest to public response. The Senate was designed for broader representation for the states with six-year terms and a slower process. Balancing competing interests was the objective by design. One body was not to be more important than the other.

The fact the US Capitol has always been the most elevated and impressive structure in Washington D.C. is not a coincidence either. It is the place designed to reflect the sacred contract of a constitutional republic. The Congress is the leadership vehicle that defines the federal government.

How did a system, so noble in its construction fall into such modern disrepute? How have we fallen to a place where members of Congress rank in the lowest level of professional esteem? The short answer is members of Congress and their political parties and allies have corrupted the system. That's the symptom. The cause of the disease is "we the people" have abandoned our duty to hold Congress accountable to the principles of the Declaration and the Constitution. Congress has morphed into a matrix of self-absorbed corruption and we have been too busy to care.

Fixing Congress

There are few things Americans agree on 90% of the time. The fact that Congress is broken is one of them. So why don't "we the people" do something to fix the problem in the most important branch of our government? Why do we always have to be kicked so hard in the head to do our duty as Americans?

History reminds us Americans are a reluctant group of leaders. Remember those cold and lonely Pilgrims back in 1620? They pioneered the art of political longsuffering. By 1776 the Founding generation had mastered the same longsuffering with the British Parliament and Crown. They admitted how reluctant people are to finally accept the responsibility to change their political circumstances, saying:

> *... all experience hath shewn, that mankind are more disposed to suffer, while evils are sufferable, than to right themselves by abolishing the forms to which they are accustomed. But when a long train of abuses and usurpations,*

pursuing invariably the same Object evinces a design to reduce them under absolute Despotism, it is their right, it is their duty, to throw off such Government, and to provide new Guards for their future security. (The Declaration of Independence)

The real kick in the head over the current political nightmare is that suffering didn't get us into this mess. "We the people" lost Congress because times were simply too good. There hasn't been a World War in two generations. September 11th got Congress to sing us all a chorus of God Bless America but that only lasted a few months. Things in America have been so good for so long that we just got on with our lives and didn't waste much time worrying about the politics of it all.

Every year the bill Congress sent us in return for our disregard got larger. Every year Congress spent more, built more, promised more. We kept mailing in our payments. Then one day we woke up to discover we had a $10 trillion debt and Congress had no clue how to back up the train.

This is the tragic reality of the American

system. The Founders carefully established the constitutional republic so that we could live our lives with very little political care. We could experience life, liberty, and pursue happiness as the primary focus of being American but not the only point of focus. We the modern people have performed more like "trust-fund babies" taking almost no care for the system that holds together the liberties we cherish. This neglect has created a vacuum of leadership that is now filled up with a very ugly mess.

Fortunately fixing Congress does not require starting over and building a whole new government. The Constitution still runs well. We have hardly exhausted its capacity. We are not getting the most out of the model because we are constantly forced to work around a broken Congress. To fix Congress we have to know what's broken. Here's where the list begins.

1) The culture of Congress is shot

2) Both major political parties are hurting the country

3) The federal budget process is killing Congress

4) Congress has lost sight of its true calling

NFL Hall of Famer, Steve Largent, went to Congress from Oklahoma. He went to make a difference for the people of his district and represent their point of view. He didn't need a political party to get elected. Everybody knew Steve and trusted him. He didn't need a paycheck or a pension. He went because he felt the duty to give back to a country that had given him so much opportunity.

Congressman Largent would walk the hallways of Congress and whistle. He carried his sport coat over his shoulder, loosened his tie and would say hello to people as they passed. He spent time calling on members in the hope of building relationships and alliances on important ideas. He took to praying for his friends and enemies on Capitol Hill.

Steve didn't last long in Congress. He has a family and a life in Oklahoma. He went to Congress and discovered most members in leadership have abandoned home. They buy homes and move to D.C. Therefore, they live the "congressional lifestyle" 24/7.

They don't fly home on weekends. There is no one waiting for them there. They go "back to the district" out of obligation, not concern. They have become Washington, D.C. and in return the Capitol City takes very good care of them.

The culture of Congress no longer supports or encourages representative government. Congress is now all about "being there." To succeed in Congress you must surrender to the institution and the lifestyle, which by its very nature, is toxic to representative government.

Congress gets a kick out of hammering CEO's for big benefits. Other than the immediate salary, Congressional leaders are treated as well if not better. They are surrounded by a city built to cater to their needs. People forget the District of Columbia is the only city legally controlled by Congress. Nobody in town is going to tick off a Member. They have private elevators, restrooms, health care, restaurants, health facilities, barbershops, dining rooms, cars, drivers, secretaries and all the rest. They are given over $1 million per session to staff and run their offices.

The story in the Senate is even worse. The Club of 100 is the most privileged club in the world. The Constitution never designed the Senate to become the House of Lords, but that's the way it runs today.

People like Steve Largent don't have a chance in that culture because the culture no longer tolerates the reality of living as an everyday American.

The political parties are the producers and directors of this Twilight Zone version of government. The parties step in through majority and minority leadership positions and define reality for the Members. They assign handlers to keep Members functioning in the Congressional lifestyle. They understand the few things Congress must do every year to stay legal. The leaders decide what political agendas Congress will execute as well.

Members quickly learn that only seniority matters in Congress. Seniority determines committee assignments and chairmanships. Popularity helps some members move up on occasion, but rarely. The political party leaders have one singular objective: control of the majority at any and all costs, which means re-electing their members first, foremost and always. What Congress is doing ceases to matter. All that matters is being in office and staying in control, because as Members are told, if you are not here you cannot accomplish anything.

One fine Senator went to Congress years ago in the hope of working on a balanced budget amendment. He campaigned on the issue and was truly committed to the idea. After his election he sat down with the leaders of his party to discuss plans to start the amendment debate. They took him aside, patted him on the back and explained, "Senator, we have no intention of ever holding a vote on that amendment. We talk about it to get good people like you elected. It will never really happen." True story.

A former Speaker once recited in a private meeting how he would bring new members into his office and let them talk to him for hours about their ideas and goals. He would bring them back as often as necessary until they had talked themselves out. He had them convinced he cared and understood and was an ally. He would then dismiss them with his blessing fully knowing not a single idea would see the light of a Congressional debate. He just needed them to fill seats so he could keep his job, perks, privileges and influence on the world. True story.

It's not about policy. It's not about the Constitution. It's not about "the American people." It's about being there and being in control. This is the culture of Congress and it is desperately broken. The political parties are picking the bones of the dying dreams of the Founders and living large in the process.

Congress is in session for two-year terms. They start in late January. The first thing the House must do by law is to pass a federal budget. They have until October to get it done. The task requires processing a budget of at least three to four trillion dollars. This monstrous task squeezes the life out of Congress for most of the year. An army of special interest groups, federal agencies, state and local governments, trade, labor, education and industry group lines the hallways and fill every possible appointment slot with members and staff. Anyone serious about getting federal money knows they must host events and fundraisers for members. The lobbyists co-ordinate the fundraising with the political party bosses so every one gets to place their money on the table. It's not a pretty process.

There are no surprises here. No company in America compares with the sheer cash power of the US Budget. So many industries are vitally linked to the process through federal regulations, grants and entitlements. The US Congress has become some strange hybrid entity which now spends most of its time picking economic winners and losers. The members are part of a voting board that divides up a $3 trillion pool of assets – every single year. And they are not at risk for a single decision or penny of the money they give away. It is all somebody else's money.

The task is impossible to accomplish with a committee of 435 House members and 100 Senators. So special senior members and their staffs take over the process. These super-players are among a handful of people who will ever understand where more than $3 trillion is spent every single year. Most members will never read the budgets they pass.

The stimulus bill controversy of 2009 was just a tiny peek into the soul of the real Congress. The members went from zero to nearly $1 trillion spending package in less than 30 days. No one read the final piece before they voted and got out of town. Forget whether it had to be done or not. Forget all the political gamesmanship. The Congressional process of spending tax dollars is broken. The burden assumed by Congress to command and control both the federal bureaucracy and the national economy is simply too big for any Congress to accomplish.

This discussion barely touches the edge of an ocean of problems in the dysfunctional body we call Congress today. Adding more testimony, symptoms, or scandals only adds to the sorrow. Congress is broken. As a corporate body it has lost its vision and forsaken its original mission.

Good people have figured it out and walked away. America's best, brightest and most accomplished leaders see no hope in serving in Congress. The people who are getting elected are walking into the best job of their lives, which means they are most likely going to do whatever it takes to keep that job. Thus the endless downward spiral continues.

The fix, fortunately, is nowhere near as radical as starting a new country. It does not require a new Declaration of Independence. The existing Constitutional structures are still on point and workable. The American equation is out of balance because "we the people" have disregarded our first responsibility of citizenship. We have failed to hold Congress accountable to the mission statement of America. Because Congress is so whacked out of shape, the rest of our government is going haywire.

Fixing the problem requires we go backwards before we can go forward; back to a mindset that set Congress on the right path in the first place.

Section Three
The Commission

Try putting yourself in their shoes. What would cause you to leave your home, family and career, get on a slow boat across the ocean and permanently move to a new continent that was a total wilderness. No one to greet you, not a single building standing, no wells dug, plots cleared, food stored, nothing but wilderness.

They didn't call them Pilgrims for nothing. They were refugees in search of a place to live free from government persecution. The issue was their Christian faith. They took the Bible too seriously for the old guards of England and Holland. They came here to live out their faith, free from harassment.

Without a deep, abiding personal faith, the New England colonies would never have survived those early years of suffering. The lessons they learned in those first winters, where half their community died from hunger and disease, were not quickly forgotten. These were intentional Christians.

The Christian Pilgrims who came to America had something in common. Whether Catholic, Anglican, Presbyterian, Baptist or something other, they were "missional." They came here to live out their faith. The Great Commission was central to their definition of reality. They taught and developed a worldview that was biblical (with wide ranging variety on specific doctrines) and wholly relevant to the world around them. They were living lives on the mission assigned to all believers in the words Jesus spoke in Matthew 28:18-20:

> *Then Jesus came to them and said, "All authority in heaven and on earth has been given to me. Therefore go and make disciples of all nations, baptizing them in the name of the Father and of the Son and of the Holy Spirit,*

and teaching them to obey everything I have commanded you. And surely I am with you always, to the very end of the age." (NIV)

When Jesus said "All authority in heaven and on earth has been given to Me…" He was not kidding. All authority means all authority. There is not a realm or sphere that is unaffected by the resurrection of Jesus Christ. He says "in heaven and on earth" meaning as high as you can imagine upward He has all authority. On the very ground upon which we stand, He holds all authority. The word He uses for "earth" is the very common word for dirt or ground. So His authority, based upon His resurrection is limitless in all directions. It covers the ground on which the Pilgrims stood as well as the ground their children inherited in the colonies. It covers the ground on which we stand today.

The original language used for in Jesus instruction to "teach the nations" is well worth analyzing. The word for "teach" is the root word for learner. Modern translations use the term "make disciples." At its core the term combines both thought and action. This term goes way beyond making "converts" or people who simply give a mental assent to believing in Jesus. A disciple is a constant learner, not simply a classroom pupil but an actual imitator of the teacher in real life. New Testament followers of Jesus are to teach others how to "do the math" by modeling a lifestyle that conforms to all the teachings of Jesus.

The Great Commission is a teaching document. Take a look at how it reads in the Geneva Bible, the most popular translation of the 1600s.

> *And Jesus came, and spake unto them, saying, "All power is given unto me, in heaven, and in earth. Go therefore, and teach all nations, baptizing them in the Name of the Father, and the Son, and the holy Ghost, Teaching them to observe all things, whatsoever I have commanded you; and lo, I am with you always, until the end of the world, Amen." Matthew 28:18-20*

The Founders had somewhere to turn for content when it came to structuring a civil government. They were students of the Great Lawgiver who had spoken to Moses and the Author of the Sermon on the Mount. We see the imprint of biblical teaching in the rationale of the Declaration and specific concepts of the Constitution. When Jesus told them to teach the nations how to live, the Founders had plenty of original material for lesson plans.

These biblical ideas worked in public practice. For generations American families, living out the teachings of the Great Commission, worked to teach, heal and serve local communities. They didn't drop their kids off at the public school for someone else to educate. They were the public school. They came here to live out the teachings of Jesus and ended up helping to build homes, families, communities, states and a nation of free people.

They were teachers. They were called to teach the nations, not simply by writing books or conducting lectures. They came to model biblical Christianity in lifestyle and community. They taught what Jesus taught at home, in the schoolhouse, the Church, and the Town Hall. They understood the Christian experience to be more than a one-time religious transaction. Teaching all that Jesus commanded included personal morality, family life, public education, art, entertainment, public policy and all of life. They did not stop their faith at the church doors.

Their worldview enabled them to understand the unique differences between civil government and the Church. They got that point but they did not fall into the trap of seeing these two institutions as inherently hostile to each other. They understood the biblical teaching that the same Creator, who established the Church, also established the authority of civil government. Each institution had their distinct purpose and role. Their worldview was not fractured by an artificial notion of sacred versus secular.

Not all the leaders of the founding era were necessarily Christian. Nor were they perfect expressions of the teachings of the Bible. Some were unholy, hypocrites, and scoundrels. Some of their children were worse. They were not plastic baby dolls. They were real, fallen, sinful humans fighting the same temptations common to man. They certainly did not all attend the same church but they did agree that certain truths were self-evident, as plain as day. When the lights on the city on the hill went dim, they didn't tear down the city and move down the hill. They repented and sought to build better lampposts.

Consider the great Ivy League Universities of today. Harvard, Princeton and so many more began as theological seminaries to train colonial students for the ministry in America. No school had the influence of Princeton College, whose President, Pastor John Witherspoon, was a signer of the Declaration of Independence. Witherspoon taught many of the men who sat in the Constitutional Convention in Philadelphia. Perhaps his best student, James Madison, became known as the Father of the US Constitution. It is impossible to separate the construction of the US Constitution from the biblical models of faith and practice established by Reformed leaders such as Witherspoon of Princeton. Even more, it was the biblical worldview that made these scholars such experts on the nature of man. Understanding human nature as they did, they were able to craft a form of civil government that worked because it was based on transcendent truth in the biblical context of a fallen world and humanity. This is the genius of the American enterprise; and it flows from a mindset trained in biblical thought.

These were America's greatest teachers. They taught their children and everyone else's children. They taught those children the Bible because that is what Jesus taught. They taught children to read so they could read the Gospel and go to heaven. They taught children to read so they could participate as citizens and not be enslaved by tyrants. When they voted for Revolution they taught by example. They went to the battlefield first. The British were out to capture, hang and quarter John Adams, Sam Adams, John Hancock, and their allies. Pastors were targets as well. Churches were burned, wives and children widowed and orphaned.

Pastors led the debate for Independence. They led their congregations into the battlefield, they supported the Constitution, and they sent forth students into every level of public service. The great difference in colonial America was the existence of an agency that was a catalyst for principle, a people group on mission to live out the teachings of Jesus Christ. That agency was the church. Take people of faith out of the historical equation of America's Founding and we would all be either drinking tea in the afternoon or speaking French today.

And What if Those Kinds of People were here, in America Again Today?

What would America look like today, if people who confess the Christian faith took the Great Commission seriously again?

Then Jesus came to them and said, "All authority in heaven and on earth has been given to me. Therefore go and make disciples of all nations, baptizing them in the name of the Father and of the Son and of the Holy Spirit, and teaching them to obey everything I have commanded you. And surely I am with you always, to the very end of the age." Matthew 28:18-20 (NIV)

What would America look like if Christians today were fully committed to a Great Commission lifestyle? The first thing that would change is Christians would cease to hide their lives in the religious ghetto. American pastors, too long content to build mini-faith-based subcultures, would have to retool their model. You cannot be the light of the world, a city on a hill, hiding out in a religious clique that primarily meets on Sundays. The calling for followers of Jesus to be salt and light is a call to relevance in every area of life.

Christians would have to connect faith and living instead of marketing Christianity as a one-time decision relating only to salvation. Making converts would have to be replaced with the much more biblical term of making "followers" or "learners" or "disciples." Millions of American Christians claim to be born-again today but live as if Christ is not Lord of anything other than the moment of their death. Their "salvation experience" is their only context for a relationship with God. There is no current reality to their faith or practice.

Churches would have to become the center of education once again in America. Pastors would teach parents who would teach their own children well. Church schools would have to accompany every American congregation and parish. Christ-followers would place the education of children as an inescapable priority of congregational life.

For any who wonder what God may think of such prioritization there is a carefully written testimony of God's heart on this matter. It is found in the 18th chapter of the book of Matthew.

If Christians in America took the words of the Great Commission seriously again the educational crisis in America would disappear in one generation. From grade school to college, the Church could provide the highest quality education to all students. There are enough certified, qualified instructors parked in congregations right now to populate education centers across the land. Think of the opportunities for college graduates to get their first teaching jobs in these new schools. There is plenty of classroom space.

Jesus never said, "Charge tuition as you teach the nations what I taught you." This act of service to the culture could make local congregations one of the most important assets in every community. Think of the money the churches could save taxpayers of all ages. Think of the jobs the church could provide for teachers. Think of the moms who dream of staying home and raising their children who could do just that.

The Church could save the academic future of the nation. What an opportunity for people of faith to reinvent education in America. Isn't that consistent with the Great Commission? Isn't that exactly what the Founding generations did once long ago?

A Unique Role for the Church in the Public Debate Over Civil Government

The American political process is broken and every honest person in this country knows it. Even the dishonest ones admit it when no one is taking notes. The process is broken because we have abandoned the Constitution and ignored our responsibilities to the Congress. In that vacuum of abdication an element has arisen that the Father of America strongly cautioned us to avoid.

In his Farewell Address, President Washington urged Americans to resist the "party spirit" of political factions. Washington was elected to the Presidency twice as a non-partisan. It wasn't until the third President was elected that political parties began their quest to control the White House. This model is critical to understand because it bespeaks the attitude of the founding generations toward political power. They did not like government – which is a profoundly American virtue. Washington likened government to a dangerous fire that needed to be constantly controlled. They viewed political office as a necessary duty to keep government under control.

Fire is dangerous unless it is managed for the common good. Who could stay that close to a dangerous fire and not get burned?

The idea of creating political clubs or networks or power bases to sway the government toward a partisan purpose was considered treasonous. These people really, truly believed in the Declaration, the Constitution and the concept of a representative citizen republic. They did not need political clubs to file their paperwork, process their petitions, raise campaign funds or handle their media. They had real lives. Politics was not their ambition. It was their turn of duty in payment for the right to live free.

Americans today have no frame of reference on any of this political history. People think the Republicans and Democrats have been around from day one. Nothing could be farther from the truth. The current political landscape is fraught with partisan peril. Washington warned us such times would come if people would place personal ambition above the common good of civic virtue. When controlling a political party becomes more important than directing political power towards just ends, America is in real deep trouble. Such is the current dilemma and the current opportunity.

Most people in America have figured out this much: they know the political parties are basically worthless. They are not members or participants in any political party. This is a critical piece of information and bears repeating. Most Americans are not Democrats or Republicans. In some battleground states like Ohio, non-aligned voters actually outnumber the total of both Democrats and Republicans by a large margin.

Political parties are irrelevant to most Americans, yet these dinosaurs continue to dominate the political landscape. Parties pretend to assemble platforms of positions on important issues. At the same time both Democrat and Republican Party leaders condemn "ideologues" who take issues or political philosophies seriously. The party platforms are nothing more than meaningless advertisement copy.

Party bosses put up candidates who stand for nothing and slap a party label behind their name when the paperwork is filed. They don't recruit people based on ideas or political philosophy. They recruit blank slates with good hair and teeth and label them like racecars. It is the biggest racket in the free world. It is everything George Washington hoped we would never become and the direct result of ignoring his specific advice to never let party politics govern American public life.

There is a way to fix all of this. What would

happen if all across the land, independent people networks began sending new leaders into public service? What if they ran for office uniformly committed to placing principle over party, first and always? What if they took a stand for the principles of the Declaration of Independence and the Constitution as it stands today?

What if people of faith refused to participate or support any political party ever again? What if they treated elected officials as people, not partisans, and refused to support any candidate based on building the power base of any political party? What if people boycotted races where no candidate stood for core principles? What if they aggressively protested the election of party hacks and instead replaced them in every Congressional race in the land with honest people willing to run and serve based on principle?

These are the most dangerous questions being asked in America today. Attaining an America free from irrelevant political parties is totally achievable. The power brokers of America don't care if you know this. They don't believe anyone cares enough to challenge them, let alone take back Congress for the sake of the Constitution. This much can be said with certainty: such a scenario is completely legal. There is nothing that prevents honest citizens from running for public office as non-party candidates. No law prevents them from running for Congress, or the state legislature or the Governor's office. In fact, most people are stunned to realize how simple it is for independent candidates to file and run for most offices. There is no law that says people cannot vote for and finance such campaigns.

What is the role for churches in all of this? There is no need for churches, as organizations or denominations, to endorse any political candidates. Churches should remain fiercely independent from candidates and parties. At the same time, Biblical leaders, should model the teachings of Jesus in holding all in power accountable to the truth. American pulpits should be ablaze with inspiration and encouragement for those willing to serve in public life and those called to support them. Pastors need to help congregants and the culture work out the match, figure out the formulas on right living in civil society. Repeating for emphasis – we are not talking about church endorsed candidates – not necessary and counter productive. There are much wiser ways for pastors and congregations to model the teachings of Jesus to a needy culture.

True Story from the Presidential Election of 2008

It was the longest Presidential election in modern history. By summer the media was exhausted with the race. The endless debates with ever revolving candidates were the height of organized boredom. In August, from out of nowhere, Pastor Rick Warren steps in and announces the Saddleback Civil Forum on the Presidency. Nobody in the media can believe Barack Obama and John McCain are actually going to spend two hours talking to a pastor in a church.

Roundtable's radio broadcast team for The Public Square® is invited to host the national radio coverage of the event. The big day arrives quickly. Out on media row at 9 A.M. the chatter begins. All the national media covering the Presidency are there and they are beyond skeptical. They cannot figure this whole Saddleback, purpose-driven church thing for starters. They keep shaking their heads asking themselves what are we doing here?

As the day progresses so does the heat. Hundreds of international media are now being scanned by Secret Service. Helicopters fly a non-stop circle above the California foothills. Police dogs and armed military guards are on constant parade. The snipers appear on the rooflines with binoculars. By 3 P.M. it is 90 degrees on the property and getting hotter.

There is one other group that keeps appearing across the campus. People dressed in light blue shirts are lending a hand, giving directions, carrying boxes, and handing out bottles of cold water. They are quiet, confident and discreet. They lead people to a lunch put on by the church. As the crowds start rolling in they work the long security lines and get people to their seats. Rumor has it these same people were in the building the day before anyone arrived, praying over every seat in the church assembly hall. Praying for whoever would be witnessing this historic first in Presidential campaigns.

In the open to the national radio program, we admit our personal skepticism about Pastor Warren being able to pull this off. For years we have seen religious leaders fall under the star power of national campaigns. We have seen them paralyzed by the moment, unable to ask the tough question or follow-up. We all knew Warren was good – but could he handle this kind of pressure?

From the opening cue, Warren took command of the stage and led the event to a level no one had seen before. He treated the candidates as human beings not partisan objects. He had a context of personal relationship with both men and it showed. Respect was the order of the day. Warren asked the best questions anyone on media row had heard throughout the entire two-year campaign for the White House. Rick Warren was, yes, relevant! He encouraged the candidates to reach for relevance and honest communication. No attacks, no point-counterpoint, none of boring nonsense that dominates politics today.

When it was over, the Saddleback Forum became an instant political classic. Syndicated columnist Charles Krauthammer called it the best political event he had ever witnessed. The Saddleback Forum was the most watched and rebroadcasted event of the 2008 campaign across cable and radio networks.

No one knows who Rick Warren ended up voting for in the November election. He issued no personal endorsement. What he did was to model what could happen if an independent agency committed to finding and telling the truth enters the arena of public policy. He modeled the teachings of Jesus at phenomenal risk.

The Roundtable has been working with pastors in this arena for over 30 years. No one has been indicted, prosecuted, sent to jail or even hassled. No one has lost their calling or congregation. In fact just the opposite happens. When pastors begin to teach a Great Commission mindset people are set free. They see the relevance of their personal faith to the world around them. They get out of the congregational ghetto and begin to act like salt and light. Lives are changed, families are transformed, community service flows, and people suddenly see the Gospel in ways they have never been able to hear before.

What about the separation of church and state? What about it? The model proposed here is no different than the same Great Commission practiced in America for hundreds of years. Congress does not need to pass a single law for this model of service to be enacted. Nothing in the model proposes the church become the government or the government submit to the institution of the church. This model is about individual citizens participating in their American birthright. It is about people of faith overcoming partisan corruption by doing good.

Can you imagine networks of people working independently across the nation in support of quality candidates who place principle over party? It doesn't matter if those candidates carry a democrat or republican or independent label. All that matters is their stand on the issues and their record of service. Can you imagine what would happen to Washington D.C. if just 50 people were elected to the US Congress who carried principle over party first, foremost and always?

Such a transformation will take an independent agency, a people group, a network of allies so dedicated to selfless service that they will give of their time, talent and finances to redeem the American system of civil government. Historically there is only one group of people who have ever been able to wrest power from the corrupt and place it back on the pathway of service. One group of people called to go the extra mile, suffer public humiliation and abuse, even lay down their lives for the good of their friends. One group who can stand among the powerful and not fall prey to the illusion of power. One group whose boss is so risen from the dead that He makes politics look like child's play. One group who can serve in the public arena but recognize their life and identity is anchored in an eternal perspective.

In the beginning the people of the Great Commission made such a sacrifice to build and establish this nation. Would to God people of faith would rediscover such a role again today, in this dark and desperate hour.

The Smaller Picture

It seems that obedience to Jesus Christ ought to be all the motivation a Christian should need to obey the Great Commission. Jesus issued the order. He said go teach, make disciples and teach them more. So why did this stop happening in modern America? Here is a brief listing of possible reasons.

1) The Church was unprepared with a solid apologetic to refute Darwin and radical evolutionary teachings in the early part of the 20th century. This was true on both the scientific front and the area of higher criticism of the Bible.

2) Reaction to the social gospel of the mid-20th century polarized evangelicals from the cultural marketplace and public policy.

3) Christian parents, pastors and educators failed to teach American history to children, leaving a void which radical secularists filled.

4) American education in both religious and state schools has propagated a revisionist

version of the separation of church and state that has further ghettoized American Christians.

5) Many Christians, fascinated with eschatology and "end times," have created an escapist mentality regarding personal and corporate responsibilities.

6) Times have been good in America and Christians have been content with a lifestyle of personal peace and affluence.

7) Some Christians have removed the word "disciples" in the Great Commission and substituted the word "converts" in its place. They have focused only on conversion and abandoned discipleship and teaching.

8) Leaders in the church have failed to lead.

Eight bullet points hardly do justice to 100 years of historical analysis, which is why we have placed a bibliography in the back of this text. Understanding how and why Christian leaders traded away the mandate of the Great Commission in the modern era is most important. The marching orders of Jesus have not been modified or amended. Since the Commanding General has not changed the orders, somebody down here must have. Justifying such behavior is always the human tendency. Sometimes it's an art form. Such rationalization in the Bible, however, is usually summed up in a very short word known as sin.

So, for the sake of obedience alone the modern American Christian should fall under the order of the Great Commission. That is the big picture of eternal significance. There is a small picture that is also worth mentioning. Societies, cultures and nations act out in real life the thoughts they hold in common. The ancient adage: "Ideas have consequences" is true on both the personal and national level.

Nations don't operate in a vacuum. If historical American principles are abandoned in civil society, the space they leave behind will not remain empty. Something or someone will try to fill that space.

The Reality of the Secular State

There was another set of ideas that travelled from the Old World to America's shore. Throughout the 20th century the vision of a secular state was experimented with across the European continent with a particular focus in the Soviet empire. In spite of two world wars and the Cold War, the seeds of a wholly secular state took root in American universities, the media, mainline churches and eventually Congress and the Courts. One century after the Bolshevik Revolution in Russia it seems fair to ask for an inventory on the practical results of the godless equation in civil society.

In 2007, The Public Square® helped bring "The God Delusion Debate" to a worldwide radio audience. The event was set at the University of Alabama Birmingham. Dr. Richard Dawkins, the world's most prolific atheist, does not debate very often but he carefully selected this venue. His goal was to participate in a public debate on atheism deep within the American Bible Belt. For almost two hours he discussed his book *The God Delusion* with Oxford Professor and Christian apologist, Dr. John Lennox. In many ways this event has become symbolic of the great debate over worldviews in the West today.

The interest in the debate and the radio broadcasts that followed are telling. The event was a sell-out. Over six thousand radio listeners responded with online comments in the first 48 hours after the event. Rebroadcasts of the debate went on for months; and The Public Square® programs highlighting this debate are still among the most downloaded programs in our archive. People are intensely interested in the discussion of core worldview issues.

Is the current rise of atheism in the West a signal that the historic Judeo-Christian ethic is doomed to the museums of history? Is the popular tide such that the West is desperate to throw off this ancient ethical platform? Has the godless equation provided a model for civil governance superior to the old ways?

The shortest answer to this last question can be found by spending a single afternoon researching the final 60 years of the 20th century. Just Google these words on the internet: holocaust, Hitler, Stalin, Russian slave camps, starvation, Soviet Union, KGB, Cambodia, Laos, Pol Pot, Red China, Mao Tse-Tung, death camps, North Korea, torture,

Castro, Cuba and total human death count. The answer is clear.

The West, operating on a Judeo-Christian model of thought, has also created horrid moments in history. We never stop hearing about the Crusades. We cannot forget the Inquisition and the religious persecutions across medieval Europe. Of course this is true history, but many of these incidents actually fueled the passion for reformation, which leads us back toward the pathway of American Liberty. There was the mistreatment of the American Indians, and we have mentioned slavery several times. All this is true. The track record of the West on human rights is far from perfect – but there is a substantive difference. The first is the body count. Count the dead bodies if you dare. Find a system more deadly to innocent humanity than the godless equation of communism at the end of the 20th century. Count the dead bodies.

Next, let's ask which of these worldviews has proven the capacity to overcome these human horrors and move forward to eliminate such injustices? The Crusades are history, though there is an eerie sense that radical Muslims would like to see a return to such hostilities. The Inquisition helped spawn the Reformation. Great Britain and America paid a horrific price for the mistake of slavery and abolished it. Americans are still working to help the American Indian today. People of biblical faith are not perfect. The transcendent ethic they hold, however, does not permit them to live with injustice very long.

The United States is far from a perfect society. Her people have made tragic mistakes across history but the Judeo-Christian ethic of American culture has never permitted her citizens to simply shrug their shoulders and walk away. The Founders saw the Creator as the Just God of the Bible. They believed all people would someday stand before Him and give account. This virtue of justice on earth, justice under the law, Liberty and justice for all is what makes the American model different from all the rest.

This eternal justice is America's greatest haunting point of conscience. It was what Thomas Jefferson admitted kept him up at night. He heard the alarm bell of injustice over human slavery and it hounded him until his death. Washington released all his slaves upon his death. He knew he was wrong. He had to make it right. It kept Lincoln awake at nights, pacing the hallways of the White House.

Where is justice in the history of godless totalitarianism? Where is the communist reparation society across Europe, China, North Korea, Cambodia, or Cuba?

Perhaps a recent comment made by Professor Dawkins best makes this point. Dawkins was a key subject in the documentary film "Expelled," produced by Ben Stein. The Professor was hardly pleased with the outcome of his conversations with Stein as they appeared in the film. He was particularly incensed with the theme of the movie. Ben Stein sought to document the linkage between atheism as a worldview and the rise of the Third Reich of Nazi Germany. The Holocaust was a particular focus for Stein who is Jewish. Without equivocation, Stein clearly connected the historical dots between the rise of atheism in Germany and the rise of Hitler to power.

Clearly embarrassed by the exposure and message of *Expelled*, Professor Dawkins went on to write several angry blogs about Stein and the film. In one blog Dawkins went to great lengths to explain:

> *"As I have often said before, as a scientist I am a passionate Darwinian. But as a citizen and a human being, I want to construct a society which is about as un-Darwinian as we can make it. I approve of looking after the poor (very un-Darwinian). I approve of universal medical care (very un-Darwinian)."*

Richard Dawkins at RichardDawkins.net, March 23, 2008

Here the most noted leader of the evolutionary/atheistic movement concedes the insufficiency of his worldview as a platform for civil government. This is a statement acknowledging the practical bankruptcy of the Darwinian movement, not by any opponent but by Richard Dawkins himself. Dawkins can find no logical bridge from atheism to civil justice. He wants to think, teach and trade as an atheist; but he wants a civil order that defies atheistic dogma and treats all people with equal justice.

What does this tell us? The radical left, at its core, acknowledges the godless equation may sell a lot of books and lecture tickets but it fails to provide a platform for real living. Man left solely to his own devices cannot construct a rationale for loving his neighbor as he loves himself. Dawkins can find no pathway from the godless delusion to practical public policy that includes self-less care for the poor, the sick or the dying.

There is however, an even darker side to the godless equation. As Stein points out in the film *Expelled*, the application of the godless equation over time results in predictable and tragic consequences in the life of a nation. The example he chooses and validates is Nazi Germany. The question he raises is: could such a disaster happen again – even in America today?

There are no tanks rolling in the streets of America yet. There are signs, however, that the growing dominance of the godless equation is beginning to tear America apart.

A Very Current Example in the Marketplace

The financial collapse of 2008 is but one practical example of the loss of a biblical worldview displaced by the godless equation. There were several complicated moving parts in this scandal that brought America to the shores of financial disaster. The creation of mortgage backed securities, credit default swaps, derivatives, synthetics, sub-prime loans and the rise and fall of the housing market are all part of "how" the problem occurred. The more important question is: "Why did this collapse occur?"

Why did people stop telling the truth to each other? Why did they permit greed to take over the process at every level? Why was Congress willing to look the other way?

Consider the track record of Congress in all of this. Congress made two huge mistakes. First they forgot the history of the Great Depression. Republicans and Democrats together abandoned the regulations keeping the financial services industry and banks from operating as a single shop. In essence they incentivized wild speculation inside the financial industries, then looked the other way as the industry created some of the craziest investment products of all time.

At the same time Congress, both Democrats and Republicans, drank the Kool-Aid on the "affordable housing" movement. In the 1990s it became cool for politicians to pretend they found a way to help people get home ownership. Find that job description for Congress in the Constitution. It was a magic show designed to prove the politicians really cared about poor people.

Congress decided to push funding, guarantees and regulations to expand the role of Fannie Mae and Freddie Mac, the quasi-government lending institutions. Congress also looked the other way as banks came under pressure from federal regulators to make more sub-prime loans to people who simply could not afford a home. This activity created new inventories of taxpayer-backed mortgage paper which the banks and investment firms started packaging and re-selling in exotic leveraged investment products.

All of this speculation helped fuel inflation in the housing markets. People started pouring into the market from around the world, chasing the cheap money and buying homes to flip, which sent housing prices in the Sun Belt sky high.

Then people started taking out second mortgages on their highly inflated properties and the whole paper chase of security backed investment products followed. Some people think the Fed had a hand in this as well by artificially deflating interest rates which encouraged more consumer debt in refinanced mortgages which drove more security backed funds into the financial stratospheres.

Then one day, gas prices hit $4 a gallon. People couldn't pay their second or third mortgage and the bubble popped. Six months later 50% of the wealth of the US stock market disappeared and the average American family lost 20% of their net worth. Millions lost their jobs and the American economy went in the tank. Why? Because telling the truth fell out of fashion. The economic realities of the godless equation struck home. In a society where telling the truth is an option, some people will choose greed and deceit instead.

Unfortunately, Congress could have stopped all this three different ways over twenty years. They were too caught up in the popularity contest of the "affordable housing" movement to discern the real threat. They were just doing what secularists do, which is, whatever feels right at the time. Congress disregarded the ancient boundary stones.

Might things have been different if the members of the US Congress had been raised up in an environment where telling the truth still mattered? Where the Ten Commandments were common currency? Instead, they have been raised in an America were "Thou shalt not steal or lie" is replaced with "Don't break the rules and if you do, don't get caught. If that fails, hide as much money as fast as you can and hire a really good lawyer." Ideas still have consequences – everywhere.

Secularists, even Darwinian atheists have consciences too. They just don't exactly know what to do with them especially if they become very successful in this life. The

Darwinian model should give them a free pass on conscience. After all a worldview predicated upon the "survival of the fittest" certainly leaves no logical room for empathy for the poor or downtrodden. Problem is -- atheists just can't live that way because it is too painful to their humanity (which bears the fingerprints of the Creator whom they deny). So the atheist academic or the "liberal" politician strives to find ways to help the poor and those farther down the Darwinian food chain. It eases their guilt over succeeding over others less fortunate.

The secularist turns to the government to ease their guilt. Unfortunately, they have no transcendent ethic, no "self–evident truths" by which to wisely help the poor without mistreating everyone else. So they default to a feeling they call "fairness." Rather than simply hand over all their money to the poor and be done with it, the secularists turn to the state. Only the state can force everyone to give some of their money to the poor and solve the problem by making things more "fair". What is missing here is obvious – the secular state has no means of balancing the competing interests of the person being taxed and the person getting the tax dollars. Lawmakers become political Robin Hoods with little logic left other than one person has too much and another too little. Fairness is in the eye of the beholder.

The Biblical model the Founders turned to answers this dilemma. The Old and New Testament clearly teach all mankind is created equal but not necessarily destined to stay that way. The Bible teaches the unique value of the individual and the right to succeed or fail based on personal choice. The Bible is clear that humans are not to be judged based upon their net worth. The rich are not to be held high (the book of James) while preferential treatment is not to be given to the poor (the book of Leviticus). The role of civil government is to provide boundary lines so that the equal rights of both the poor and the rich are secured. Government is not designed to guarantee the result of the choices made by either the rich or the poor.

The secularist complains such a system can never eliminate the poor. The answer to which is "Exactly!" Government is not designed to eliminate poverty. Nor is government designed to guarantee wealth. Read the Constitution. There are worse things in life than being poor, like being a slave to a totalitarian state. Since government cannot guarantee success, without violating the property rights of others, the outcome of economic decisions must be left in the realm of private citizens. They will fail or succeed on their own. Government protects their opportunity to try and their right to their property.

What about the poor? In some cases the people pass laws to direct assistance through collective action. Those programs seldom are effective in doing more than making it easier to stay poor. President Bill Clinton led the charge against this mindset in the 1990s claiming the "end of the welfare state." In America a "poor" person is entitled to tax-funded housing, food, health care and education. What if a person of higher means goes broke? America also provides a "softer landing" through bankruptcy laws to protect total devastation. In spite of more than 50 years of these policies and trillions of tax dollars taken from working Americans, poverty is still with us – because government action cannot completely eliminate the consequences of all human choices.

Does this mean America should stop trying to help the poor? Of course not. The message is there must be a better way to help than collectivism and government programs. Did communism or socialism eliminate poverty in the Soviet Empire or across Europe? Are there more poor people per capita today in America or in Russia? How about Cuba? Once again, let's take a simple inventory. Which system creates more liberty, private property, opportunity and wealth?

Acknowledging the dangers of greed requires acknowledging something about human beings that modern secularists don't teach kids in school anymore.

The Founders built the American system of government based upon a biblical understanding of human nature. Humankind was created in the image of God; therefore every person has value that cannot be denied. Every individual, however, is born equally fallen in a fallen world with the potentiality to do both good and or evil. This is the nature of man, which prompted Madison's famous quote "If men were angels, we would need no laws."

The modern secularist has no time for such discussions. Madison's doctrine on the relationship of law to fallen human nature never reaches a classroom or a law school lecture anymore. When American school children grow up and become members of Congress they are clueless on the worldview and operational dynamics behind Constitutional law. In Congress they just make it up as they go along, counting on the Courts to straighten out the mess. The problem is the judges on the Courts went to the same law schools as members of Congress and are equally clueless as to the foundational principles of justice. They rely instead on prior Court rulings called precedent. That's what they teach in law schools today; not what the Constitution says, but what the Courts have ruled over the past few hundred years. So we have a classic case of the "blind leading the blind" and both falling into a ditch.

This is the applied economic reality of a society that has abandoned the historic principles of the Declaration of Independence and the US Constitution. This is what happens when we teach children the secular revisionist view of history for fifty years or more. They grow up clueless but sincere with the potential to bankrupt the world with the best of intentions.

George Washington tried to warn us that government was a dangerous fire. He recognized that the light and warmth of fire comes at the cost of consumption. The fuel for government activity is always human capital and human liberty. Why? Because government has no assets, no manufacturing plants, no inherent wealth. The American government at its core is a set of documents in the national archive. The only money the government has is money Congress takes from people who have earned it by making things, mining things, growing things, or serving others. The government can only give away that which it first takes away. As the role of government grows human liberty and capital are consumed in the fire.

The first collapse is now all around us. Can the next one be prevented? Can anyone help pick up the pieces and bring Americans back to first principles?

The Pathway Home

> *Stand at the crossroads and look;*
> *Ask for the ancient paths,*
> *Ask where the good way is,*
> *And walk in it,*
> *And you will find rest for your souls.*
> *Jeremiah 6:16 (NIV)*

> *Come to Me, all you who are weary and burdened, and I will give you rest. Take My yoke upon you and learn from Me, for I am gentle and humble in heart, and you will find rest for your souls. For My yoke is easy and My burden is light. Matthew 11:28-30 (NIV)*

How long is the journey home? How long will it take for the nation to turn back in a positive direction? Is there enough time, energy, and money, left to make the change? What is the plan?

First: Some Very Personal Advice

These are all good questions but they may not be the right questions. Perhaps the place to start is by asking: Do we honestly believe the words of the Great Commission?

> *Then Jesus came to them and said, "All authority in heaven and on earth has been given to me. Therefore go and make disciples of all nations, baptizing them in the name of the Father and of the Son and of the Holy Spirit, and teaching them to obey everything I have commanded you. And surely I am with you always, to the very end of the age." Matthew 28: 18-20 (NIV)*

Looking in the mirror comes first. Do we believe all authority in every realm of current life and in the life to come belongs to Jesus Christ? The first step on the way home is acknowledging my personal failures and repenting. It starts in the mirror.

For example, does my confession match my actions. I talk a great game about the Lordship of Christ over every area of life but do I live the same life in the marketplace that I do at the church house? Do I treat the people I work with the same respect? How do I handle my enemies as well as my neighbors and friends?

The list goes on but you get the point. Finding our way home is first personal then corporate. It is a work that happens from the inside out. The lights have to be on inside first if we are to offer any light to the world around us.

Next, the task of American renewal begins at the kitchen table, or counter or wherever you sit down everyday alone or with your family. People of faith in America are starving to death in their spirits. God reminds Moses that human beings cannot survive on mere bread alone. Jesus quoted the same passage stating:

> *Man does not live on bread alone, but on every word that comes from the mouth of God. Matthew 4:4 (NIV)*

We cannot have an impact upon a nation starving for truth if we are suffering from the same famine. People of faith need to reconnect with the source. One reason the Church has lost its impact as salt and light in the culture is believers have neither the flavor nor the light of God's word in their lives. We can't offer what we don't have. We can't teach everything Jesus commanded if we don't have a clue as to what Jesus taught. Here is a simple suggestion: spend five minutes every day reading a portion of the Gospels. The best way to learn the teachings of Jesus is to read what he said. My old philosophy professor taught us years ago to read a portion of the Gospels every night at bedtime.

The next step is to get a copy of the Declaration of Independence and the US Constitution and read them both. Surprise again – it doesn't even take an hour to read them both. Pretty amazing. You can order a copy of both in the companion book to this series by logging onto aproundtable.org. Get the material and keep it handy. Put copies around the house and in your backpack and briefcase. Take it when you travel. Read it on airplanes. You'll be surprised how different America looks when you begin to analyze things from the perspective of these source documents. Be your own teacher.

Next, we urge you to begin to pray for America. Praying for those in authority is not a suggestion, it is a commandment in the New Testament (see 1 Timothy 2:1-4).

St. Paul wasn't just messing around when he urged us, "first of all" to pray for those in authority. Praying for them means we have to know who they are by name. By logging onto aproundtable.org you can get the names and all the contact information for your state and federal elected representatives. What would America look like if everyone who claims to be a follower of Jesus actually obeyed this commandment every single day?

Pray for politicians? How do I do that? How about if we just pray for them as people – for just a minute or two everyday and ask God to have mercy on their lives? "Pray for them? I don't even like them? Do you know who my member of Congress is?" God does. And here is a news flash – in our form of civil government – where we get exactly the kind of people in Congress we vote for – God holds us accountable for putting them in office. So we better be praying for them everyday. "But they are the enemy!" Ok, so what does the Bible teach about praying for our enemies?

Once we are fully engaged in this discipline personally, then we have to encourage it in the church. I know that may sound crazy to you right now. "We the people" have to help pastors remember to pray on Sunday morning for America. Yep, it's true. Just ask yourself when the last time was you heard your Pastor or Priest pray out loud for specific elected officials on Sunday morning. They don't teach this in Seminary. It is not being modeled much by denominations or mega churches. You won't find many books on this. All of which might give us a clue as to why America is in so much trouble.

We are actually suggesting you become a pest on this matter. Not an unkind pest, but a person who simply will not take "no" for an answer. After all, how are we going to hold members of Congress accountable for their actions in office if we are not willing to hold fellow believers accountable to pray for those in authority. Some people use the "prayer request" cards in the pew racks every week to send in a request to the pastor to pray for the nation. Many lead prayer in their life group classes and small group studies. Some go to elder and deacon boards with resolutions. There is no reason to be anything but kind and joyful in this pursuit but it is a commandment, a direct order and critically vital to the mission.

Try This at Home but Don't Try it Alone

Nothing replaces being genuinely truthful in our personal core. It is difficult to keep on this track if you are the only one on it. Pray that God will bring a fellow traveler on this path. We all have the temptation to begin to carry this burden for America on our own backs. Doing so will accomplish little other than a broken back. No one can carry this burden. It has to be laid off to the Lord in daily prayer and reading in the Scriptures. Pray someone will come along to help remind you of this fact constantly. The Roundtable is always putting together people networks of support. The aproundtable.org site is free and updated every day with you in mind. There are words of encouragement from radio broadcasts on the site that you can tap into every day as well. We also host policy briefings and major events to help you meet others who truly care. There are other organizations that are offering help as well. Get connected. Don't try to carry this burden alone.

Next Steps

Learn more backwards and forwards. When we teach the American Mission© class in schools and congregations it is always fun to watch people get new books about old subjects. The booklist from the 13-week course of study is really good. We have known most of the authors for years. Their books are written for normal people who want to learn more. So we encourage you to fall in love with American history and learn all you can going backwards from today about this nation. The story is intoxicating.

Next, we have to get informed on what is happening at the Statehouse and the Capitol. Getting to know the local school board and city council also makes sense.

We used to tell people to read the newspaper

everyday. That advice has changed slightly. We are still big fans of local papers but they are disappearing and dropping in quality. They are still a good place to start, but the Internet is also a very good investment for news. In fifteen minutes you can learn a lot.

What about cable news and talk radio? We are very careful with both those media. It is important to remember that most radio and TV networks are in business to make a dollar first and foremost. They are "news-entertainment" outlets. They exist to create ratings because ratings magnetize ad dollars. They are all – read ALL – content-controlled according to management design. They all are biased toward a single objective: ratings. It is good advice to trust none of them without verifying anything they tell you.

What about the media personalities you like and agree with? Be glad you've got a friend; but don't get goofy. They don't know you. You don't know their contract. You don't know if management just sat them down today with new polling numbers and told them to pump an issue for sweeps rating week.

Another thing about electronic news and talk personalities is this: most of them have never done anything in public policy—other than talk about it. They have never stood in the rain registering voters or circulating a ballot issue petition. They have never sat around a table and crafted legislation or testified before a House or Senate Committee. They have never seen the inside of federal court, let alone had their ideas tested face to face by the Supreme Court. They get paid very well to talk about something they have never done. A few of them are former state officials or members of Congress. They have a bit more credibility but the average talk show or cable "host" couldn't hit a policy curve ball if it was thrown to them underhand. So don't let these people get too far under your skin. Roundtable's National Legislative Director, Melanie Elsey, always tells us "Eat the fish, leave the bones." Dr. Jeff Sanders of the Liberty Committee reminds daily radio listeners, "Don't let anybody rent space in your head – including us." God gave you a mind for a reason. Don't be afraid to use it. Learn all you can about the issues you care most about but, "eat the fish and leave the bones."

Next it is important to learn the process of how state and federal legislatures work. This sounds like a lot of homework but it is not. Don't buy into the illusion that the lawmaking process is difficult. It is not. It was designed to be part-time work for average citizens. When we the people stopped paying attention the career politicians mucked it up by turning it into a career path.

It has often been said Congress would be a better place if we picked 535 random names from the phone book and appointed them every few years. Members of Congress REALLY hate that line. Yes, it is an overstatement; and a bit unfair, however – there is a kernel of truth in that phone book illustration. Civil government is not supposed to be hard in America. Incumbents and their party bosses make it look hard because they want to keep you out of the process. When you know what is going on you begin to show up and ask honest questions. That takes time; and they are busy people. When you start to really understand the process you may even decide to run for office someday or encourage someone you know to run. That's competition and threatens the political class. Don't let that bug you.

The next step is becoming an ambassador. Really, me an ambassador? You don't get a car and bodyguard, sorry. We are talking about you getting to know the four or five people who are legally responsible to represent you at the Statehouse and on Capitol Hill. Your job is to represent them as well, as you pray for them everyday and hold their name and family before a merciful God. You can do this with one-minute of your day: one simple minute.

They need to know you exist. They need to get an email, letter and phone call from you on a regular basis that says: "We are praying for you." If you are a local pastor, the Director of Roundtable's Shepherds Staff has a few more suggestions. Pastor John Bouquet of Ashland, Ohio has been doing this ambassador work with elected officials for years. He is in constant contact with local Mayors, Commissioners and Legislators. He views them as part of his extended congregation. He is not pushy or a pest. He simply is loving and faithful. He prays for them daily and every now and then stops in to say hello or calls them directly to ask, "How can I pray for you today?" That's it – no strings attached.

The policy connection is here. These elected officials know Pastor Bouquet cares about a lot of issues; but they know he cares about them as people more. When these officials get a mailing or info about issues from Pastor Bouquet he is writing to inform them of a concern. He has earned the right to be heard. Many times the politicians disregard Pastor Bouquets' point of view and vote the wrong way. They will still get the same phone call next month that says, "How can I pray for you today". When one of his extended congregation of elected officials gets sick, Pastor Bouquet visits them in the hospital. When there is a funeral he tries hard to be there, even if just for a moment or two. This man is being salt and light by modeling relational integrity to leaders. His model ministry can be duplicated by Christian ambassadors across the nation.

The rest of us non-pastors can do

something very similar. We may not be called to quite the pastoral level; but we can get to know our elected officials by visiting them at public events. We can stop by their public offices that we pay for with our tax dollars and say hello. We can send them a birthday card every year. We can be ambassadors of honest care to these people and their staffs.

There is a catch right? We do this so when a big issue comes along we can hammer these politicians with forceful arguments because we have access, right? Wrong. If you asked that question in your mind or out loud please go back to the beginning of this section and start over. Politics is not simply about force and pressure. It is about truth and light. We hold legislative elections every two years in this country. That's a built in accountability no politician can escape. The goal of being an ambassador is to help those in public office grow spiritually and to help them understand the principles of the Declaration and Constitution.

"What if my elected officials are real jerks? I tried this and it didn't work." That happens a lot, don't worry. Keep praying and keep sending a note now and then. "I supported their opponent who lost last election now nobody will talk to me. I am the enemy." Ok, keep praying and send a note every now and then and don't forget the birthday card. Just because they treat you like the enemy changes nothing. We are called to pray for our enemies.

Are you getting the picture here? A true follower of Jesus Christ, partnered in the Great Commission never gets off mission. A true follower is always a teacher, always modeling the right response that flows from the teachings of Jesus, regardless of results.

Quick side note: this is easy advice to write and real tough to live. After 30 years of trying none of us score 100% on this discipline so don't get discouraged. We are all called to be ambassadors by the only One who is risen from the dead. This work gets done in His power not ours.

The Final Step is: We Have to Send New Players Onto the Field

Have you ever considered that 535 people could begin turning this nation around in two years? Better yet, just 51% of 435 members or 218 people could change Congress and the nation. If there were 60 members of the US Senate who did the same, the entire Congress is turned around.

From a nation of 300 million we are talking about finding and electing 278 people who are willing to stand for the Declaration and the Constitution. Do you know why that hasn't happened? Actually, just the opposite has occurred. In the last 10 years the radical left, led by monstrous funding from George Soros and others has taken control of the US Congress. They did not do so by funding the Democrat Party. They did it by utilizing hundreds of independent left wing organizations like Emily's List, Fund for a Progressive Majority, MoveOn.org and ACORN. They built their own people structures and took over the Congress and the White House.

The great irony is this: this radical left cabal does not represent even 10% of the US population, yet they are now in control of the Congress and the White House and soon the Courts. How in the world could the rest of America sit idly by and let such a fractional minority take over?

For a generation people of faith have sat in the stands and been faithful fans in the arena of public policy. We have spent millions in political contributions paying for the right to cheer for the people actually playing the game on the field. In the end, in spite of all the investments, we are still only spectators watching from the stands unable to touch the ball, move it down the field or score any points. And we are the most pathetic kinds of fans as well. No matter how often our "team" drops the ball, calls a stupid play or throws the game to the other side, we keep buying the tickets and showing up.

In short, the biggest mistake conservatives and people of faith have made in the modern era was to trust the Republican or Democrat Party. Isn't it about time to put a new team on the field that can win?

Here is a simple plan to change all that. What if you and your friends and their local congregations, civic groups and allies decided to find people to run for public office? What if you plugged into independent resources to help train these new leaders and teach them the ropes?

Yes, this sounds foreign to our ears. We have been raised up in the illusion that only the two major political parties are allowed to run people for office. This has always been the job for "somebody else" to do. Our abdication of this most basic civic duty has created an elite political class that is now poised to destroy the foundations of the Constitution and this representative republic.

Please read these next words most carefully: We are not talking about starting a third party, an independent party or any party at all. We are proclaiming the end of political parties as vehicles for political participation. They are not necessary and largely a waste of time. In this digital era we don't need two gatekeepers into civil government. Those days are over.

That's how the change begins. Every two years you make sure you have a candidate for State Rep, State Senate and US Congress. It does not matter if they are Republican, Democrat, Independent or non-aligned. You help find them and get them connected into the process. NO, you don't wait for permission from the political parties. If your recruits want to be party boys and girls, find someone else. There is a subtle but huge difference here. These new leaders can run with a party label if they must, but they don't have to do so. The choice is yours.

Your candidates must be willing to run their campaign and vote in office independent of the party bosses and machines. Principle over Party. They must be their own people independent of party domination. If not, then everyone is just wasting time. You and your allies are sending independent candidates into races regardless of party identification. If you can win with a principled candidate filing as a Democrat or Republican or Independent – it does not matter. Support quality people in all parties along with quality people who can run and win as Independents. You are a free agent, doing the work of responsible citizenship.

At first the party bosses will hate every step of this. You will be operating outside the box they have worked so hard to build and therein keep you trapped. They may get nasty and call you and your friends names. Or they will be politely patronizing and then stab you in the back. Professional politicians don't share well with others or play nice. So here is your chance to man-up or go home. If you want to see America turned around then you have to keep doing the right thing regardless of the "Pharisees" who currently make up the ruling class. The voters can't stand these party bosses and they will be more than willing to give your new candidates a fair hearing.

The first few elections will be tough but not nearly as tough as the War for Independence against Britain. Then you will win a few races and suddenly the whole picture will change. Here is the key: You are not trying to "take over" anything. You are simply walking out your responsibilities for the system that was given to you in the first place. All political power ultimately resides in "We the People". All we are doing here is showing up for work and cleaning house.

Too tough to do today? Why? Companies, churches and schools recruit and train leaders and staff every single day of the year. In this model we are recruiting and training leaders willing to love their neighbor by serving in public office. The fact that Christian people have missed this opportunity to serve for so long is pretty amazing.

This is not too tough for the radical left in America today. They have been doing it since the 1990s. So how have we come to the place where people holding the agenda of the radical left actually give more, work harder and provide leaders in public life while people of faith just sit in the stands and groan?

Here is an example. A group of people got together on this plan a few years ago in Youngstown, Ohio. Fed-up with Democrats dominating the Mayor's office and Republicans having no chance to win, these independent citizens found an excellent Independent candidate. They built a coalition of community leaders and independent PAC's like the Liberty Committee to support the Independent candidate who ran, won, and has been a good Mayor. They sent the party bosses packing and took care of business as independent citizens who care. This same model can work in any major city in America and every Congressional district as well.

The average population in a single Congressional district is about 650,000 people. What would happen if every two years a handful of churches in each of the 435 House districts worked together to recruit and train someone to run for Congress? Maybe they recruit three candidates and they run as Democrat, Republican and Independent. Let the best person win. The other two can run for another office or come back and try in two years. Do you think out of 650,000 people there is one qualified candidate who could run and win with the right training, backing and help?

What if this principled candidate gets beat? So what? Run them again and again until they win. The very fact than an incumbent is being legitimately challenged in a district changes everything. The impact is huge and sends a powerful message of accountability. What if you are comfortable with the current incumbent? If you are blessed to have a Representative or Senator that actually stands for the Declaration and Constitution, then hold onto them – but not for too long. It is a fact that the longer your good member stays in Congress or at the Statehouse the worse the corroding influence of the bureaucracy will be on them. If you have a good member, plan on replacing them every eight years or two terms maximum in the Senate. You will be saving their lives. Career members of Congress don't ever come home and if they do, nobody recognizes them anymore. Honestly, it is not healthy for Members, voters or the representative system to paralyze rotation in office. If you have a great House member, help them run for a different office after eight years. If you have a great Senator, let them come home and run for Governor, or take one term off and enjoy their pension plan. You can re-elect them later.

Do we back Republican, Democrat or Independent candidates? The answer is yes. The single strongest element of this entire effort is the fact that people of faith, following the Great Commission model truth in this arena. The truth is—there is no need to participate in forwarding the agenda of any political party.

There is no value in picking a party and trying to influence it by a singular focus. It has been tried before, multiple times and it always fails. It defeats the whole purpose of reaching the culture and winning the public debate for ideas that work. The founding principles are more important than partisan agendas so people of faith must be talking to everyone in the process. Picking a Party and trying to run a short-cut strategy of taking over Congress with a single party is just plain stupid. Winning the culture and moving candidates in who will vote Principle over Party is the only way to win in the long run.

Talk show hosts don't like this strategy. They want the world divided up between Republicans and Democrats. They do so because their model of entertainment always requires a good guy versus a villain. In the talk show world everything is point-counterpoint, the bigger the argument the better the ratings.

This approach doesn't work. So why do we keep playing into that strategy? Back in the 1960s the US Congress was a very different body. The influence of conservative thought permeated party boundaries. It was not uncommon to find Democrats from the South and Republicans voting together on a number of issues. The principles crossed party. We have to get back there again. It may take the election of a dozen or maybe a hundred people to Congress who run as Independents and knock off corrupt incumbents. Those independents will have a remarkable opportunity to leverage principle into the Congressional debate.

If the ideas of the Founding Era work, and we know they do, then those ideas are American ideas. We should be ever diligent to offer those ideas to all candidates, all leaders and all political parties. We should hold all candidates, Democrat, Republican and Independent accountable to the Declaration and the Constitution.

Political parties do not care about party platforms anymore. They exist to raise and spend money on themselves and to get their people elected who can then spend more of other people's money. They will do anything to win and control seats. They are exactly what George Washington predicted they would become. We have to find leaders willing to serve independent of the corrupt party structures. We have to build the people networks to sustain those leaders. This can be done, it must be done, and it is the only way home for America. Independent PAC's like The Liberty Committee are working on just such a plan. (www.libertycommittee.com)

This last step, of changing the players on the field, is the missing element that modern conservatives have never embraced. Their mistaken allegiance to the Republican Party has wasted an entire generation and millions of dollars. Their intense issue battles have been mostly wasted effort because of bad people in office who will never do the right thing no matter how many letters and phone calls are sent to them. If the people of faith in America fail to break this cycle of failure, the wanderings in the wilderness will continue for another generation and America will suffer irreparable harm. If we don't change our strategies today, there may be no America left to change tomorrow.

This text has focused on three key words:

the Constitution, the Congress and the Commission. There is a fourth that also starts with the letter "c" that determines whether the message of renewal contained here ever becomes a reality. Short of embracing this word, all that has been said is simply conversation. Embracing this word and applying it to the very same principles held by the founding generations is the pathway home for America. It is the final word: Commitment.

America started right. America was built on a solid foundation. America has corrected grievous errors in the past by returning to founding principles. We have once again lost our way and are far, far away from home. The pathway back for America is not an impossible journey. We cannot get there by simply acknowledging the truth or just praying about it. We have to change. We have to get up off our collective tail-ends and start walking and working to get home. That takes commitment.

Enough talk, it is time for action. The journey begins with a commitment to a continual life of daily prayer and devotion to the study of the Bible. We will have to change the way we spend our time and our money. We will have to commit ourselves and our futures to the mission field of America – to once again living out the model of being truly Christian in thought and deed right here in our own back yard. We have to own the responsibility to field new leaders in Congress and the Statehouse. Given how far this nation has fallen we will feel like Pilgrims again, which is never easy. Truth has never been easy, but Jesus Himself promises us power if we seek Him in this mission. He promises us His Presence so that we will not be alone, not ever, not until the very last day of earth. The commitment is ours to make.

The Great Commission remains.
Home is waiting…

For the eyes of the LORD range throughout
the earth to strengthen those whose hearts are
fully committed to him.
II Chronicles 16.9a

Appendix

About the Author

David Zanotti grew up in a family of six in a small home outside Cleveland, Ohio. His father was a WWII veteran. His grandparents were Italian immigrants.

Mr. Zanotti attended Cuyahoga Community College, Mt. Vernon Bible College, Mt. Vernon Nazarene College, and did graduate work at Ashland University. He left his family's manufacturing company in 1985 to join the Roundtable.

David Zanotti currently serves as President/ CEO of the American Policy Roundtable. He also serves as President of Roundtable Freedom Forum, a legislative organization and is Chairman of The Liberty Committee, a federal Political Action Committee.

In 1989, Mr. Zanotti began hosting a news and commentary broadcast, The Public

Square®, which has become one of the longest running daily feature broadcasts in America. Today, The Public Square®, co-hosted with Wayne Shepherd, is heard across the nation in both the daily and weekend editions and via the Internet. In October 2007, The Public Square® hosted the national radio special, "The God Delusion Debate" featuring Oxford Professors John Lennox and Richard Dawkins. In 2008, Mr. Zanotti and Mr. Shepherd co-hosted the historic national radio broadcast of The Saddleback Civil Forum on the Presidency, moderated by Rick Warren.

Mr. Zanotti and the work of the Roundtable have appeared on ABC News, NBC News, CBS News, PBS Frontline, The McNeil/Lehrer Report, Fox News, MSNBC, CNN, CNBC, C-SPAN, National Public Radio, The National Press Club, *The Wall Street Journal, USAToday, The Washington Post, The Washington Times, The New York Times, The Chicago Tribune, The Dallas Daily News, The LA Times, The San Francisco Chronicle, Time, Newsweek, US News and World Report,* the BBC and several foreign media services. He also bumped into Larry King at a coffee shop in Beverly Hills, but has yet to make an appearance on Larry King Live.

Mr. Zanotti has been blessed in marriage to the same wonderful wife since 1976. Together, they have worked to raise three children in the hope of faith, family and liberty. His favorite movies are all comedies. After more than thirty years in public policy, he would still rather have lunch with Billy Crystal or Bill Cosby than attend a meeting at the White House or on Capitol Hill.

Books written by David Zanotti:

God Won't Vote This Year (2007)
The Commission (2009)

Both are available from The American Policy Roundtable.

About the American Policy Roundtable

A generation ago, a handful of "ordinary people" began meeting together out of a growing concern for America. Their conversations, prayers, and research led to the founding of an "extraordinary" public policy effort that would blossom into the American Policy Roundtable.

Recognizing that America is - at its core - a commitment to ideas and principles, the Roundtable was established with the mission of restoring the historic Judeo-Christian principles to American public policy. The Roundtable seeks to fulfill this mission statement by meeting three core objectives:

1) Rekindling the American Spirit -- by telling the story of Liberty everyday.

2) Building networks of leaders, who will help others join in the adventure of responsible citizenship.

3) Overcoming evil in civil society by promoting positive alternatives in public policy.

To accomplish these objectives the Roundtable model is built upon state-based public policy organizations, established in strategic states, all working to change America from "the bottom-up." Each state-based Roundtable organization serves under the auspices of the Board of Trustees of the American Policy Roundtable.

Impacting public policy is a process that requires multiple areas of activity. Competing in the realm of ideas is critical, but alone cannot prevail in a Constitutional Republic. Good government also requires constant vigilance in the Legislative and Judicial process as well as a constant flow of new leaders to serve in public office. The Roundtable model incorporates the necessity of this "three-pronged" approach to public policy.

Federal and state laws require certain

types of organizations be established for these specific purposes. The Roundtable is a 501(c)3 education and research organization. Roundtable Freedom Forum is a 501(c)4 organization focused on legislative activity. The Liberty Committee is a non-affiliated federal PAC that works on selected candidate campaigns. Each of these three organizations are vital components in the state-based model pioneered by the Roundtable.

The American Policy Roundtable is an independent, non-partisan, not-for-profit organization. No funds are solicited or accepted from any political parties or candidates.

American Mission Book List

Defending the Declaration
Gary Amos
Providence Foundation, August 1996
ISBN: 978-1887456050

The Light and the Glory
Peter Marshall & David Manuel
Revell, September 1980
ISBN: 978-0800750541

Christianity and the Constitution
John Eidsmoe
Baker Academic, August 1995
ISBN: 978-0801052316

Miracle at Philadelphia
Catherine Drinker Bowen
Back Bay Books, September 1986
ISBN: 978-0316103985

How Should We Then Live?
Francis Schaeffer
Crossway Books; 50 Anv. edition, March 2005
ISBN: 978-1581345360

God Won't Vote This Year
David Zanotti
American Policy Roundtable, December 2007
ISBN: 978-0977963218

That Hideous Strength
C.S. Lewis
Scribner, May 2003
ISBN: 978-0743234924